See the Child, Love the Child, Know Yourself: Now Teach

SEE THE CHILD, LOVE THE CHILD, KNOW YOURSELF: NOW TEACH

Selected Essays

ELAN LEIBNER

Waldorf
PUBLICATIONS
RESEARCH INSTITUTE FOR WALDORF EDUCATION

Printed with support from the Waldorf Curriculum Fund

Printed by:

Waldorf Publications at the
Research Institute for Waldorf Education
351 Fairview Avenue, Suite 625
Hudson, NY 12534

Title: *See the Child, Love the Child, Know Yourself: Now Teach*
    Selected Essays
Author: Elan Leibner
Editor: Patrice Maynard
Layout: Ann Erwin
Proofreaders: Tertia Gale, Ruth Riegel
Cover image: *Gold Collection #5* by Ursula Stone, oil on canvas

Table of Contents

Introduction   7

Authenticity in Education   9

Contemplative Work in the College Meeting.   16

Language, Art and Deep Study   31

The New Impulse of the Second Teacher's Meditation . . .   40

Between Our Demons and Our Gods   58
    Human Encounter in the Light of Anthroposophy

Introduction

For the six years that the Research Institute for Waldorf Education (RIWE) was fortunate enough to have Elan Leibner as the editor of the *Research Bulletin*, a striking confluence of practices and consciousness from both the Pedagogical Section Council of North America (PSC) and that of more standard research ideals was possible. Elan was and is the chair of the PSC and has stimulated attention and effective practices in spiritual research out of his own Waldorf teaching experiences and out of his own research. "Responsible innovation," as Elan Leibner has named and encouraged it, along with colleagueship through earnest study practices, are among the fruits of this unusual combination of tasks. They offer the shedding of bright and nourishing light onto the efforts of Waldorf teachers, and all teachers.

Collected here are the essays he has written for the *Research Bulletin* during this fruitful convergence of RIWE with PSC. Contemplative practice and its place in Waldorf education and spiritual research, study practices toward deeper community building, mindful incorporation of meditative approaches in faculty meetings, authenticity in teaching, and pursuit of self-knowledge of our highest and lowest selves as teachers are some of the pictures and ideas Elan Leibner offers in this gathering of essays and lectures. Reading along through these essays, you will discern that his descriptions of innovative approaches to study and colleagueship were developed while identifying cutting-edge research for RIWE that supports the approach of Waldorf education.

It is a satisfying opportunity to be able to publish these articles collected in one book that offers inspiration and vision. It has been a delight and a privilege to read them again to prepare this manuscript. The articles were excellent in the issues of the *Research Bulletin* where they first appeared and are even better as the book they have become. The urgency of the need to weave spiritual truth into all that we do as human beings, to incorporate this practically into everyday life, especially as teachers, and the brute counter-force that materialism presents as we strive to do so make a book like this a relief and a quiet, mighty support. That we never give up is, perhaps, the most important building block of our teaching efforts. The book assists in this most important, difficult, and ineffable goal.

– Patrice Maynard
Hudson, New York
May 2019

Authenticity in Education

The following essay is adapted from an address delivered at the graduation of Sound Circle Center's Class of 2011 in Seattle, WA.

Dear graduating class, colleagues, families, and friends,

We are gathered here on the eve of Pentecost, and though what I want to bring today is not overtly related to this festival, I would say at the outset that the image of people gathered in a circle, inspired by a spiritual fire, turning outwards and devoting their lives to the spreading of an inwardly experienced truth is very much what stands at the core of Waldorf education as we should strive to practice it.

The path you have chosen is as noble and worthy an undertaking as there is. Of course, you know that nobility and good intentions carry you only so far. Effort, perseverance, patience, talent will all play a major role in what lies ahead. Your destiny will bring you to certain situations, and we all pray that you will rise to meet them in the right way. The specifics we do not know in advance. But here is what we do know:

The crises of our time are primarily crises of authenticity. In the food we eat, in the thoughts we articulate, in the societal structures we have erected, in the manner we produce, consume, and discard goods, most surely in the education that most children receive today, we have divorced ourselves from both the reality of nature and the nature of reality. Authenticity means that the spiritual and the material, the ideal and the manifest, are in harmony. We call people authentic when their actions and words convey the indelible thrust of their individualities, norms and traditions (while respected) notwithstanding. We are often willing to forgive them social transgressions of tactlessness or absentmindedness precisely because we sense an authenticity that is precious for being so rare. In their words, as Emerson noted, we hear our own rejected thoughts.[1]

The appearance of a person or thing will only then be deemed authentic when we behold in it the underlying spirit. From authentic art, conveying experiences at once intimately personal and vastly universal, to authentic reproductions of ancient crafts, employing the original methods and materials, to such mundane examples as authentic cuisine, meaning utilizing the ingredients and methods of its nominal region, we demand an honest connection between that which is perceived and that which can only be thought.

Authenticity, while often proclaimed, has seen its star decline. The reality that was once evident, then remembered and finally only understood, seems a quaint relic. The conception of nature as whole has been replaced by a conception of nature as a collection of things. The conception of the human being as an embodiment of a divine spark has been replaced by a host of "nothing but"s. The heart is nothing but a pump; the self is nothing but an epiphenomenon of matter, and so on.[2]

Indeed, with reality as it was once understood in decline, we pride ourselves on the incredible sophistication of the new, virtual reality. Virtual means "almost," so we have almost reality, and it increasingly seems preferable to actual reality. Children have virtual pets and virtual farms and virtual friends, and parents like them because a virtual pet does not soil the rug and virtual friends can be monitored with filters and web cams. A child who plays, if we can call it that, in the virtual playground will not get run over by a car or fall and break a leg. I don't want to go on, but my intention is clear, I think. When I say that the crisis of our times is a crisis of authenticity, I mean that the underpinnings of reality have lost connection with their manifestations, and we look at these manifestations as accidental arrangements, then fancy we can do better. We can rearrange the manifestations for greater convenience and profit.

The sad thing is that we are actually meant to do better, just not in the way we have been understanding that possibility. Doing better means doing authentically, doing in accord with the spiritual essence of the human being and of nature. What is urgently needed is the understanding that nature can no longer heal us on her own, and in fact needs us in order to be healed herself. In the words of Dennis Klocek, Mother Nature is now old. She needs her children to care for her.[3] Rather than rearranging the manifestations of reality for convenience and profit, we need to rearrange convenience and profit to accord with reality.

We will have to learn, but also help create, the virtue of reality—a newly emergent, humanized reality—so that virtual reality will not be the final word. We will have to develop heart intelligence so that artificial intelligence is not the final word. To the World Wide Web we must add the World Wise Web, a web of human relationships for those who seek both wisdom and its application.

And where does this idea lead when we look at education? Human nature is not different in this sense from the rest of nature. Convenience and profit now dictate how we approach young human beings, too. On the one side: "Global competition means we have to produce more engineers and programmers!" On the other: "My child's feelings were hurt, so he doesn't feel like completing his craft project before graduation." The idea that authenticity means identifying a child with his or her own self, not with a profit motive or emotional chicken soup—that idea is almost nowhere to be found.

It would be so very tempting to pronounce here that Waldorf education is the answer to the quest for authenticity in education. Follow the curriculum, best practices, AWSNA self-study guidelines for your school, Sound Circle instructors' methodologies, and voila: Authentic education!

Of course, understood correctly, that Waldorf education is the answer to the quest for authentic education is exactly what I will be saying. But I would like to characterize Waldorf education more as a verb than a noun or an adjective. I would like to ask you to "waldorf" with your students rather than "give them a Waldorf education." Using nouns as verbs is known as verbing. I once saw a cartoon that said that "verbing weirds the language." It seems apt, however, because in making Waldorf into a verb we come closer to its spirit, and hence to its potential authenticity. I believe that, in the long term, we may be better off ditching the name altogether and just empowering ourselves to educate. The curriculum that has been taught in Waldorf schools is wonderful, wise beyond compare. But even this remarkable achievement can become a burden if the person teaching it is slaving under it like one whose spirit has been shackled by tradition.

What is the alternative to predetermined do's and don'ts?

See the child, love the child, know yourself: Now teach. This is the immensely simple and so endlessly difficult maxim of authentic education. For what it includes, and also for what it excludes, it comes close to pedagogical anarchy if applied selfishly—and to a truly human education when applied with humility and courage. Let's look at those exhortations. *See the child, love the child, know yourself: Now teach.*

12

See the child.

Every tuft of hair, every gesture, every speech impediment or artistic talent is a sign. A sign in the sense that words are signs, pointing towards meaning. But words are someone's words, and someone else has to understand them. The tuft of hair, the tilted head, the nervous laughter—they are the speaking of the child's invisible spirit. You have to permeate them with the light of your mind, to read the signs together into speech if you are to see the child so that you can help connect the spirit with its instrument—that is, if you are to foster authenticity. The language anthroposophy has given you should help as a set of principles to organize your seeing. Used well, it fosters true beholding. Used badly, it's an obscuring curtain, a nominal classification that absolves you of the charge to see.

And how will you know whether the child is seen, and grows authentic? The child will let you know. Ask every evening, and the answer shall be given unto you.

Love the child.

Though he may not love you—at least not initially. Love even the child you cannot grow to like. Liking is of the soul. It half sleeps and cannot lightly be convinced to vacate the soul dwelling it acquired in the murky past. But love is of the spirit. You may let your actions flow towards what the moment asks of you even if every disliking strand of you begs permission to mock, or cringe, or run away, or blame heredity, nutrition, media, traffic and weather together, or the Montessori kindergarten for all that ails the child. Be like the angel, your angel, that has stood by you despite all that you have done to make yourself unworthy of angelic love.

And how will you know if you have loved? Love is a peculiar force. The more you give away, the more you have. If it grows within you, you have been giving it away. The child you have loved will form a bond with the Self she means to be. This need not mean without trouble, all confident and happy. But she will confirm the fact that you are on her side as she seeks to find her way. Your relationship will bear the stamp of your love for her, rather than your like or dislike of her. It will grow authentic.

Know yourself.

"Know thou thyself" is an ancient call, an ancient riddle. Who is to know whom? It directs us to the mystery of cognition, which is well beyond the scope of this address. Today I would like to speak of it in a humbler sense. Know yourself, that you are also an embodied Self, that in this embodiment you have talents, weaknesses, abilities, and disabilities. Launch into the teacher's journey with warmth, enthusiasm, and determination. Please, please do not attempt to do everything as well as the teachers in your teacher education courses have demonstrated. You were given examples of lessons by people whose special strength is music, or drawing, or movement. They were not all as musical as the musician or as talented a storyteller as the storytelling master. What made them good enough to be invited to teach you was that they developed their gifts.

So in your first year or two, concentrate on developing and nurturing a teaching style that builds on your gifts. Are you a poet? Teach math in rhyme, geography through the poetry of the regions you wish to explore, and history with ample samples of the dramatic, the epic or the lyrical. Are you a lover of nature? There is English in the trees and mountains of your community, physics in the meandering brook, and history in rocks and wildlife. You are given the freedom to meet your students' needs in a manner unique to the uniqueness of the day and tasks at hand. When you have built a teaching hut from which to set forth every day, then surely you can work on developing those talents that you did not receive as a gift of destiny. Nature's lover can engage his dormant love of music, and the poet can brave her fear of colored chalk or movement. Live on the edge of the comfortable, enlarging it.

But first get comfortable. Ask for help. Accept the help. True help is of the same nature as the teaching we are looking for; it seeks to help you find your voice. At times it may simply mean that someone else will carry music, nature, or poetry for you. As a seasoned teacher I can promise you that people like me long to be asked for help by their new colleagues. Take advantage of them. A mentor worth his oats will strive to help you teach the way you ought to teach, connecting your gifts of destiny with the task at hand: that is, to teach authentically.

So know yourself, and love the child you've learned to see. With your colleagues, form the Waldorf Pentecostal circle of those who seek self-knowledge, a new seeing, and Love in its noblest, most spiritual sense. Together, you will know more, see more, and love more.

Now teach!

ENDNOTES
1. Ralph Waldo Emerson, "Self Reliance" from *Selected Essays* (New York: Penguin, 1985).
2. For an enlightening discussion of the absurdity of these "nothing buts" see Georg Kühlewind's essay, "Theories of Consciousness" in *Feeling Knowing* (Fair Oaks, CA: Rudolf Steiner College Press, 1993).
3. Dennis Klocek spoke these words during a seminar for mentors held in Seattle in April, 2011.

Contemplative Work in the College Meeting

Introduction

The possibility of developing a successful collaborative, spiritual-leadership model depends on the participants' ability to become, collectively, a vessel for wisdom greater than their own. This wisdom may reveal itself in fundamental insights (Moral Intuitions, in the language of *Intuitive Thinking as a Spiritual Path*[2]), creative visions for addressing the ramifications of those insights (Moral Imaginations), or plans for incarnating the visions into the specific reality in which the school is operating (Moral Technique). While individuals may well be capable of achieving some of those steps on their own, the fundamental idea of the collaborative model is that single capacities can be enhanced through collaboration. Furthermore, collaboration may indeed allow individual capacities to reach their full fruition by providing the listening attentiveness that often holds the key to sounding out one's inherent potential.

A second facet of this model is the spiritual dimension: The group is engaged with spiritual beings, and this engagement implies spiritual effort. This dimension is the one with which this essay is primarily concerned. The third facet is the element of leadership; the model is meant to offer guidance that can be followed by the school. Engaging in spiritual work, even in a collaborative fashion, is insufficient in itself; the group still needs to provide leadership. The guiding imagination for this model, at least in Waldorf schools, is the so-called College Imagination, delivered by Rudolf Steiner at the inception of the *Study of Man* course in 1919.[2]

Steiner describes a circle of teachers, with each member's Angel standing behind him/her, placing a hand on the teacher's head, and allowing strength to stream forth. Steiner later refers to this as "the spiritual meeting of each individual with his angel." This strength allows imaginations to stream into the pedagogical work. Above, Archangels are gathering the strength, which "has been enhanced through uniting with all the others," and make "a chalice of courage" out of it. Into this chalice, Archai (angelic beings of a higher order than the Archangels) allow a drop of light to fall. Light is a spiritual term synonymous with wisdom, and the process of helping teachers become recipients of light in the manner indicated by the College Imagination is the main subject of this essay.

Crucial for the idea we are trying to develop here is Steiner's description of how the capacity to receive intuitive wisdom ("drop of light") is preceded by the forming of a vessel ("chalice of courage"), and how this vessel is composed of "what is coming to birth through the spiritual meeting of each individual with his angel." It is clear that this *spiritual meeting* is the very foundation of the collaborative spiritual model being inaugurated. I would suggest that this meeting consists of inner, meditative work.

The space here is too limited for a full discussion of the nature of inner work, yet a few germane points can be singled out. One such point is what Steiner calls "the gate of humility."[3] When one practices humility in the pursuit of wisdom, an enhanced ability to relinquish a supposed ownership of ideas, or to allow better ideas to improve and/or change what had been brought into the discussion follows. The very notion of reaching for higher wisdom suggests that there exists a wisdom higher than what one may presently possess. Absent this practice, one may cling to one's "own" ideas out of an all-too-human vanity. But one learns on a meditative path to release one's attachment to ideas-as-possessions. Ideas are placed at the service of others, or, in this instance, of the leadership process. This is, I believe, what Steiner meant when he spoke of the Archangels carrying from one individual to the other "what is coming to birth through the spiritual meeting of each individual with his angel." I will refer to this later in this essay as "freed spiritual substance." It means ideas that have been freed from ownership. Together a group of such ideas can serve as the preparatory vessel, or chalice.

A second contribution of the inner path is the notion that one's colleague is also "on the path." Sensing that the other, too, is working to become a better vessel for the spirit increases the willingness to be patient with his or her idiosyncrasies, since there is hope that the gaps that yawn between colleagues may narrow in the next minute (or the next year). Colleagues are less likely to view each other as forever destined to remain the same. Sustained over years, colleagueship in Waldorf schools needs the optimism that the hope (indeed the anticipation) of change brings. Group processes can otherwise suffer "occlusions of the light" born of the blindness people always have for the "better angels of [each other's] nature." The willingness to see—and the practice of seeing—the good in one's colleagues forms an essential aspect of what Steiner calls the reverse ritual, meaning the elevation of the striving community to the company of spiritual beings.

The most important contribution that a meditative practice offers a collaborative spiritual-leadership model, however, is the presence of concentrated, receptive attentiveness. A meditative path begins with exercises to improve the focus of one's attention. Once attention is focused on a "something," we can remove that "something" and have a moment of becoming aware of attention itself as a form-free *capacity. Empty, receptive attention* is the pre-requisite for new ideas. When a group can develop an "empty attention," when it is available and willing to receive new ideas, it has also developed an essential aspect of the "chalice of courage." The surest way for developing this collective capacity is for the individual members to engage in developing their own capacities.

We can say, therefore, that for this collaborative spiritual-leadership model to succeed, the members of the leadership group should be actively engaged in a meditative practice. It is indeed my view that most of the failings of Colleges of Teachers in Waldorf schools can be traced to the absence of sufficient meditative work. Freed spiritual substance (created and freed through the individuals' meditative efforts) is then missing for the chalice-forming activity of benevolent spiritual beings, and the members of the College are left with nothing but their too-limited earthly powers. "Drops of light" can be difficult to receive without the spiritual chalice having been formed. Even when individual members receive new ideas, the receptivity of the group is not sufficient for these ideas to become fruitful.

Assuming that the collaborative-leadership model depends on individual meditative practice, a new difficulty arises. An individual inner path is difficult to establish. During teacher-preparation courses, many a student focuses on other aspects of the profession, and the habit life of a meditative practice is not firmly established. Afterwards, many new teachers make an attempt, encounter the inevitable obstacles, and essentially give up on a regular practice, perhaps replacing a cognitive path with prayer. Such individuals may even be quite gifted teachers, but their capacity to serve as contributors in a chalice-forming process is undoubtedly compromised. Sooner or later they come up against obstacles (some alluded to here, others elsewhere in this publication) and, absent the tools developed through inner practice, they may either burn out or burn others out. Burnout is essentially the consequence of an inability to renew oneself, and renewal, in this context, means tapping the source of new ideas.

Sometimes a school will have a few "old timers" who have an active meditative life that allows them to carry the spiritual essence of Waldorf education and serve as pillars for the work of the College. But as they begin to retire or move on to other chapters in their biographies, a kind of spiritual implosion results. Colleagues, parents, and former students may remark that the school "doesn't feel the same anymore." Whereas the implied change is not necessarily bad, it may point to a kind of active absence, if you will, of that "something" that made the school work more deeply in the past. Peripheral teachers are asked to become central pillars and leaders of chalice-forming practices, yet they lack the foundation of an independent spiritual practice. This possible picture is not to suggest that every old-timer is a meditative practitioner, or that newer colleagues are not meditants, but merely to point towards a phenomenon that may illustrate the role of meditative practice in the collaborative spiritual-leadership model.

If we agree that contemplative practice is crucial to successful leadership in Waldorf schools, and that establishing this practice is fraught with challenges, are there steps that can be taken to support individual teachers attempting to develop such a practice? Practicing exercises and even engaging in contemplative work in groups can be of great help for those trying to launch an individual meditative life. The reason might be that successful concentration is often easier to achieve when undertaken with others. Whereas as physical organisms we are always separated from one another, in soul and spirit we are more woven together; the efforts of those around us can help draw our spiritual capacities in the desired direction. There are legitimate concerns about doing this work in groups, and some of those concerns will be addressed below, but once individuals experience what a concentrated state "feels like," they are more likely to persevere in attempting to reach it on their own. Put another way, once we know what we are looking for, we may have more patience trying to find it. Even for people with many years of faithful practice, doing contemplative work together can provide enhanced strength, often leading to new and surprising directions in their individual work. Hearing how others have approached a verse or an image is helpful when the sharing is done with the proper restraint, but actually practicing *that* approach with them seems to offer a gift, a benefit born of their many years of practice. One feels "gifted" by one's colleague, and deeply thankful.

In my own experience, a College that had struggled for years to overcome personality-driven conflicts and endless debate was transformed within a matter of weeks into a far more receptive and cogent leadership group once various forms of inner work were practiced during the opening segment of meetings. In my view this occurred because the shared substance of the opening segment was already uniting the individuals' higher capacities by the time discussion of school matters began. The College members had engaged a demanding text or an exercise, had spent time reflecting on the content or the experience, and had dedicated themselves and their efforts toward the wellbeing of the school. A shift had occurred in their consciousness and mood. The daily hubbub of teaching and the experience of interacting with people on the level of intellectual, informational consciousness had been replaced by a period of intentional dedication at the contemplative level. The ground was then prepared for a different kind of interaction.

It might be argued that shared substance can also be created through ordinary study. The essential difference, however, is that in contemplative work the shared substance is actively taken into each individual's inner life, and the attempt is made to understand the "content" at the level from which it originated. Rudolf Steiner (or another spiritual researcher) had experiences across the threshold, and then had to "clothe" those in words; our task as students is to proceed in the reverse direction, starting from the words and reaching across the threshold to the experience. A conscious effort is undertaken as well to invite something more than one's ordinary understanding to enter the process, something that transcends what the individual is already thinking. In some "regular" studies, the discussion rarely, if ever, transcends the informational, content level. This informational level of consciousness is the level of arguments, not the level of humble receptivity indicated by the chalice imagination. But a group of people that has engaged in a period of contemplative practice is primed for a meeting that can become something more than "just a meeting." We can get a feeling for the difference from a lecture Steiner gave on February 28, 1923:

> And if several people come together with what they
> have from their everyday consciousness, and don't with
> full sensitivity lift themselves up to the supersensible
> world, if such people meet together merely to hear the
> language of the supersensible world in the everyday
> state of soul, then there is an infinitely great possibility
> that they may begin to argue, because in the most
> natural way they become egotists in relation to each
> other. ...If people take their normal soul life into
> their supposed understanding of the teaching from
> higher worlds, then of course this leads to egotism and
> argument.[4]

Objections and Dangers

Some people might object to the idea of contemplative work in groups because "Rudolf Steiner did not do this kind of work in groups, and therefore it is not appropriate for us to do it." This kind of orthodoxy is dangerous, since it restricts anthroposophy to precedent rather than allowing it to meet the moment, but it also misses an important factor: the effect of Rudolf Steiner's personal presence at the first Waldorf School. Anyone who has worked with a genuine spiritual researcher (e.g., Jørgen Smit or Georg Kühlewind) knows that listening to such a person is in itself a meditative exercise. His thoughts blaze a trail of light that has to be followed by attentiveness unlike the one we use for ordinary intellectual content. In *How to Know Higher Worlds* Steiner says of the communications of the spiritual researcher:

> For such instructions are culled from the living inner
> word...they are themselves gifted with spiritual life.
> They are not mere words; they are living powers.
> And while you follow the words of one who knows...
> powers are at work in your soul which make you
> clairvoyant.[5]

When Steiner assembled the first Waldorf School teachers and instructed them, the "content" was given in the *Study of Man* lectures and other such pearls of higher knowledge. When he attended their faculty meetings, the discussion was sometimes entirely practical, but then would veer into insights that could not be properly received without subsequent meditative reflection. Steiner assumed that the teachers were meditants, and he gave them "content" and even mantras to support their work. He spoke directly about the need to meditate on the "content" of his lectures:

23

And it is especially interesting to allow everything I have presented today to work on you; let it invigorate you. ...If you bring all these things together and form mental images of them in *active meditation*, you can be sure that the vigorous power of ingenuity you need when facing the children you are educating will be kindled in you.[6] [Emphasis mine]

In the absence of a spiritual researcher to guide the teachers in a school, other forms of support for the faculty members' meditative work may well be needed, and the exercises discussed here could be one approach for providing such support.

Contemplative work in groups does present some legitimate dangers, however. Those dangers are born of the temptations that beset the path toward higher knowledge, and just as the presence of others may help along this path, it can also exacerbate some of the pitfalls. A few of the potential dangers are discussed below, and a group that intends to pursue this kind of work is encouraged to discuss these and reach a set of agreements to mitigate them. This set of agreements may be spoken at the beginning of each session or in some form be mentioned as a reminder to those present.

Danger: Contemplative work in a group infringes on individual freedom by coercing a person to engage in it when s/he might not want or feel able to do so. Such a person would either engage in the practice against his/her better judgment, or, if the practice is expected of everyone, leave the group altogether. One possible solution is to engage in this work before the official beginning of the meeting; another option is to allow members to excuse themselves; a third possibility is to allow members to be present quietly without engaging in the work. Each group should decide how to handle this difficulty.

24

Danger: Since work in groups is easier for some, individuals might choose to replace their personal practice with group work. This is not what anthroposophy should promote. Anthroposophy is an individual spiritual path first and foremost. The group should discuss what, if anything, the members might commit to doing outside the meeting. In my view, some form of commitment to individual practice should become one of the agreements.

Danger: Individuals sometimes suggest or imply that they have achieved more in their practice (or during the group exercises) than is actually the case. This brings an element of untruth into the very heart of the school and creates a mood around the spiritual practice that is harmful rather than helpful. Absolute honesty, integrity, and humility must pervade every aspect of this work. Of course, these attributes are generally expected of College members, but a special emphasis should be placed on them in this context.

Danger: Details of people's individual spiritual life might be shared during parts of these sessions, leaving those individuals open to a breach of trust. Thus what was offered in full confidence can end up coming back in a completely different context. If the group discusses the question of moral character (see below), then additional aspects of vulnerability are placed in trust. Some form of agreement regarding confidentiality is needed. This might include provisions regarding (not) sharing with members absent from the group, and of course (not) sharing with non-members, including spouses. It cannot be overemphasized how important this agreement is for the long-term health of the group.

If these four dangers, in whichever form College members opt to address them, are countered, then I believe the group may safely engage in contemplative work together. As already mentioned, it is a good idea to have a short reminder of these agreements at the beginning of each session. Obviously, in specific circumstances additional agreements may be necessary, and every group is free to create and amend any agreements it makes.

Examples of Formats and Practices

A group will usually assign an individual to prepare and lead the sessions. This assignment may last for just one meeting or for an extended period of time. The group has to determine the scope of the leader's mandate in terms of choosing the themes and formats of the sessions. Some experimentation is recommended so that the comfort zone of a particular group can be established. Some groups need parameters set in advance (e.g., length of time for each session, length of assignment of leading the sessions, restrictions on the themes for meditation, and review format), while for other groups a more open-ended beginning is preferred. Even in open-ended beginnings, a review of the practice should be planned within the next two or three months, if not sooner. Inner work is delicate, and we do not want members of the group to have growing frustrations or resentments over issues that could be resolved through a review. A sensitive leader will seek to navigate the practice so that individual concerns may be addressed before they become festering problems, but a regular review is also important.

There are many ways to engage with contemplative content, of course. For the purpose of the work discussed here, three steps seem basic enough to be regarded as fundamental:

- Centering: concentration exercise/s to focus the attention
- Engagement (with the theme)
- Review

There are other steps that could be considered. It is possible to begin a session with a dedication. The members dedicate the work to the school/organization and renounce personal gain or attachments. Another step that can have a profound effect is "stooping through the gate of humility." Members remind themselves of their own shortcomings and of the notion of a wisdom higher than one's own. By remembering Steiner's exhortation to take three steps in the perfection of one's moral character for every step taken in spiritual development, participants can think of three moments in the past day/week/month during which they fell short of their moral ideals. One then resolves to place three balancing gestures into the world during the following day.

However the session is opened, the first step in the actual work is centering. There are many examples of concentration exercises in the anthroposophical literature. Of particular note for all three of the steps mentioned above is Georg Kühlewind's little booklet, *The Light of the "I."*[7] It contains a wealth of practical guidance and examples of exercises, as well as advice on dealing with obstacles. The period of concentration cannot be too long because of time constraints, but it should not be shorter than a minute. A two- to five-minute timeframe is usually sufficient. Members may concentrate on a simple man-made object, the movement of the second-hand of a clock, or other non-interesting subject. The point is that the attention is focused through one's effort and not through the object's being interesting.

The second, central part of the session is engagement with the theme. This theme may be a verse (such as one of the Teachers Meditations), an image (such as Michael and the Dragon, or the *Rose Cross*), a theme from a lecture (such as the physiological locations of auditory and visual processes described in the third lecture of *Balance in Teaching*), or a phrase (such as "Wisdom lives in the Light"). The leader suggests a manner of working with the theme for that session, and the group engages. One example of working with a theme is to "condense the verse" into its verbs only, so that the meaning is sought through the movement of the verbs. If that is successful, the verbs, too, can be removed and the whole theme is held in wordless attentiveness. As with all meditations, the theme itself has to be removed after it is beheld wordlessly. Most people are not able to have an empty attentiveness for more than a brief moment, so one returns to the theme, reduces it, and tries to reach the empty state again. It is important that one is not worried about "getting somewhere" during this period, but simply engages as far as is possible on that day.

Another possibility is to imagine that one is writing the verse: Each word is "selected" from amongst other words in the "meaning vicinity" so that this word is chosen as opposed to that one. Thus "*Spirit* beholding" at the beginning of the second Teachers Meditation is chosen instead of "*soul*" or "*inward* beholding." Next, "*beholding*" is chosen instead of "*meditating*" or "*remembering*," and so on. The experience of "writing" the verse in this way gives one an intense level of identification with the text, much as one would have when writing a poem. One can contemplate a line, a section or an entire verse in this manner. Again, once the meaning has been explored, a wordless beholding should follow, and finally a removal of the theme itself.

There are many possibilities of working with themes, and the two chosen above should be taken only as examples to illustrate the process. Steiner's books, as well as those of other anthroposophical authors, offer an abundance of themes and instructions. In addition to the Kühlewind book mentioned earlier, Dennis Klocek and Jørgen Smit have also published excellent instructions. It is left for each group to determine, or leave it to the leader to determine, how long the engagement should last. A general suggestion is ten to fifteen minutes.

When the engagement period is over, some review should occur. The review can be brief or prolonged, done inwardly by each member or through a verbal exchange, but it should happen. It allows each member to recognize what just transpired and to thank the spiritual world for its help. If the review is conducted through conversation, the tone should be restrained and reverent. Questions, insights, and suggestions may be shared, but the conversation should not lapse into casual chitchat. There should also be a clear ending for this part of the meeting. The session leader or the meeting chair should clearly separate the meditative segment from the rest of the meeting. It may even be good to stand and stretch, or read a verse, in order to transition out of one mode of conversation and into another.

Concluding Thoughts

Waldorf education is nearing the hundred-year anniversary of its founding. In some respects, it is a mature movement with traditions, standards, and habits. In its essence, however, it is meant to be ever the newborn creation, mediating the intentions of spiritual beings directly into the physical world. I believe that the sine-qua-non of Waldorf education is the teachers' meditative lives. Unless a conscious path is cultivated for spiritual beings to support the human being, "Waldorf" will become ever more a noun, a thing. It is a bit better when used as an adjective, but perhaps we should aim to make it into a verb. We should aim "to Waldorf," meaning to actively connect a child to his/her pre-birth intentions, to work in such a way that our work is "a continuation of what higher beings have done before his birth" (*Study of Man*, Lecture 1). I hope that the path offered in this essay can be support for this intention.

ENDNOTES

1. Rudolf Steiner, *Intuitive Thinking as a Spiritual Path* (Hudson, NY: Anthroposophic Press, 1995).

2. Rudolf Steiner, *Study of Man* (Forest Row, Sussex, UK: Rudolf Steiner Press, 2007).

3. Rudolf Steiner, *How to Know Higher Worlds* (Hudson, NY: Anthroposophic Press, 1994).

4. Rudolf Steiner, *Awakening to Community* (Hudson, NY: Anthroposophic Press, 1974).

5. See note 3 above.

6. Rudolf Steiner, *Balance in Teaching*, Lecture 3 (Great Barrington, MA: Anthroposophic Press, 2007).

7. Georg Kühlewind, *The Light of the "I"* (Great Barrington, MA: Anthroposophic Press, 2008).

Language, Art and Deep Study

In the Spring 2011 Issue of the *Research Bulletin* (Vol. XVI No.1), I published an article titled "An Outline of a Study Methodology." The article described a four-step protocol for studying demanding texts. In Fall 2012, while preparing to describe this protocol to an organization unfamiliar with Steiner's work,[1] I realized that there is a whole background to this approach, a background that I had taken for granted while writing and speaking to Waldorf colleagues. After a few conversations, the idea that there may be some benefit to an explicit description of what was assumed in the original article motivated this second piece. At the end of this article, I have re-presented a brief description of the methodology itself. The spoken character of the original presentation has been left largely intact.

The Twofold Nature of Language:

In every language what is originally a connected and unified whole is broken into two parts: signs and meaning. Written and spoken languages are only the clearest examples of meaning-making. Body language, facial expressions, and the use of color, tone, symbol, clothing, and every other manner through which we communicate thoughts, feelings, and attitudes—all follow the same principle. On the one hand there are perceptible signs (letters, gestures, sounds, and so forth), and on the other there are never-perceptible meanings. No meaning is ever sense-perceptible. Obviously, words written in a language you do not understand convey no meaning for you, and culture-specific gestures (e.g., "thumbs up") are not always understood by persons in a different culture. The meaning is found not *in* the words (written or spoken) or gestures, but *through* them. Words also don't have a finite meaning. That is why new thoughts can be expressed with "old" or familiar words, and also why those familiar words can be misunderstood in their new arrangement.

Secondly, for a language exchange to exist, we have to have a speaker and a listener to the speaking. I use the terms "speaker" and "listener" here in a broad sense; "author" and "reader" are also applicable. The speaker experiences some meaning, produces a set of signs, and the listener has to interpret those signs and arrive at the intended meaning of the speaker. We can speak of *mis*communication only because the assumption is that proper communication *could* have taken place, that is, the speaker and the listener could have ended up understanding the same thing (the same meaning). An exchange assumes two entities capable of producing and understanding meaningful signs. We cannot speak of a miscommunication in the conversations that I have with myself in the shower.

Summarizing, then: in language we have perceptible signs, hidden (non-sensory) meaning, a speaker, and a listener. This summary sounds simple, but it points to fields of study that extend well beyond the theme of this article. We will restrict ourselves here to the study of texts, but the principles we explore have wide and far-reaching consequences. They point towards a view of the world, including the natural world, as having the nature of a text, rather than being a world of objects, and to a spiritual discipline aimed at reading this text rather than reducing it to non-meaningful formulations. A text implies both interconnectedness amongst the separate "words" and an author. There is a human and natural ecology implied that we have to leave largely in the background.

The Four Levels of Language:

For simplicity and clarity, I will discuss written and oral language here, though other forms of speaking in the sense just mentioned would also apply in most instances. Also, importantly, the levels are not separated by stiff boundaries. Most uses of language flow between levels, and there are innumerable midpoints as well. Think more watercolor wash than oil paints. The transitions are not sharp.

1. The first level of language is what we can call *Information*. Examples of this level are owner manuals, ordinary directions, and road signs. The essential characteristics of informational language are that: 1) the meaning is finite, and 2) it is intended to be comprehended entirely and with as little effort on the part of the listener as possible. In fact, the success of this level of language is measured by precisely these comprehension-criteria: did the reader fully understand how to operate the camera after looking at the manual? Did the driver find the destination? Did the soldier understand the command? The aim is to have as little ambivalence in the text as possible, with no room for opaque language. If the listener does not understand the communication readily, then it has not been a successful exchange. Anyone who has ever tried following poorly given directions knows how unsatisfying they can be. Conversely, a well-written set of instructions makes the work simpler to accomplish and more successful. In short, on the informational level we want the signs to reveal the full meaning and the meaning readily discerned by observing the signs.

2. The second level of language is what I would like to call *Discourse*. This is the level on which the exchange between the participants is ongoing, the roles of speaker and listener change at least occasionally, and which is open for new meanings to

emerge while it is ongoing, and perhaps even later. The archetype of this level of language is a *good question*: Even the questioner does not fully know the answer, and there is a common sense that the realm of meaning is fluidly entering the exchange, appearing as signs in the perceptible world. The discourse differs from the informational level in its quality of unfinished-ness. New ideas are possible and even welcome. However, one requirement of this level (that distinguishes it from the next level) is that the realm of meaning should still emerge as fully expressed as possible, so that the participants still end up with a common, *thinking* understanding of the meaning. Less of the meaning is conveyed at the initial stages of the signs than was the case on the informational level, but we want it, in the end, as fully fleshed out as possible.

Just this once I want to point to an intermediate level between the four main ones, so the basic fourfold structure is not understood as being too rigid. For example, an *argument* can happen entirely on the informational level, but it can also reach towards the level of discourse by becoming a conversation. The main difference has to do precisely with the willingness of the participants to consider new possibilities. Inasmuch as they strive only to prove the rightness of their pre-existing views, the argument will remain informational in character. But where there is openness, a discursive level can be reached. Similarly, when appeal is made to emotions through the use of charged terms, the next level is woven into the experience, albeit often in its debased aspect.

3. The third level of language is **Poetry**. With poetry we are entering a level of language in which the meaning is no longer comprehensible through thinking alone. There is always a quality of feeling that is added, and that has to be experienced

by the listener (or, more commonly, reader) if the poem is to be "fulfilled." A good poem captures a quality of feeling in such a way that the reader can find it as well. A bad poem is still a set of signs of the poet's experience, but those signs give the reader no meaningful experience. With good poetry there are qualities that cannot be expressed in informational-level alternatives. It captures something that has to be felt, and the feeling-comprehension of the reader has to capture the feeling-expression of the poet. We are now dealing with a level of meaning-making that requires what Georg Kühlewind calls *cognitive feeling*. We will return to this shortly, but for now, note that the signs already convey the potential meaning less fully than at the level of discourse. We can point to legends and myths as forms of poetic language. Their meaning is multi-layered and requires effort and inner participation on the part of the reader. A good novel is also poetic in this sense; the distinction between prose and poetry is not important here. When signs are used to manipulate the emotional state of the listener on behalf of the speaker's agenda, we meet the debased form of the poetic level. This is how most forms of propaganda and advertising operate.

4. The fourth level of language is ***Demanding/Meditative Texts***. On this level, the signs are but tips of immense icebergs (or, better perhaps, "light-bergs") of meaning. The writer or speaker has had a fully conscious experience of profound spiritual truth, and has tried to cloak it in words that, however, can only be understood as a kind of code. There are communications of this nature in all esoteric traditions. Comprehension on this level of language is intensely demanding of the reader or listener (hence the designation), and requires an exceedingly mobile level of inner experiencing. One of its most salient characteristics is that it cannot be understood unless the reader is willing to give up

the certainty that pervades the simpler realms of language. By demanding this flexibility, the text can lead to comprehension that transforms the reader. When we talk of using art in deep study, it is for texts written at this level that we are directing our efforts. There are many forms of harm that can befall those who try to understand demanding texts on a simpler, especially the informational, level. For example, some religious groups try to interpret Scripture as an informational text, i.e., literally. Inevitably, the result is a cocooned and in-bred framework of untenable concepts, such as the idea that the world was created in six twenty-four-hour periods.

Art:

As already mentioned in the case of poetry, art is also a special case of meaning-making. The artist utilizes a medium (color, form, sound, movement, words, and so on) to clothe in sense-perceptible vestments an experience from the realm of meaning. This experience need not have been fully conscious, but it must, if it is to be meaningful to others, have some communicable dimension. Great art, said Paul Klee, does not reproduce the visible; rather, it makes visible. We can ask: makes *what* visible? In the sense of our line of thought, it is *meaning* that is made visible (or audible, etc.). But this "making visible" has the special quality I mentioned earlier: perceiving it requires a kind of feeling. This is not feeling in the sense of emotions. It is not a me-feeling, but rather a feeling for the qualities present in the artwork, a feeling of "that." This is why art appreciation can grow over time and even be taught. At first we have me-feelings: I like it, or don't like it, and so on. Later, we can put these emotions aside and contemplate the art on its own terms: we can live into the yellow streams and the black lemniscate almost as though we were painting them, streaming with our consciousness into the work in order to discover its ineffable qualities. The stories of its creation, the technique, the materials, the composition, all of these can add layers of experience that enhance our comprehension of what "it says." Of course, we can still like it or dislike it, but we can understand, or rather experience directly, its qualities regardless of our emotional response.

Artistic creations, as with the poetic level of language, are nearly always incomplete; they require an audience to experience them in order to become "fulfilled." Almost all artists will tell you that the most highly valued opinion for them is the opinion of their peers. When someone else who speaks your artistic language finds your work good, there is a sense of completion that even selling it for very high prices cannot give.

There is an exception to this general principle, and it is an important part of the process I want to describe next. When art is created in the process of studying demanding texts, the creator of the art can also be its audience, and in that sense it is complete because one person can be both the artist, or speaker, and then later on, the listener. We can tell ourselves artistic stories. This rarely satisfies artists in other situations. But the artistic phase of the study does not have to satisfy others; it is a step in a ladder of comprehension that each participant creates for him/herself. We do not have to be good painters, eurythmists, or poets to use those arts meaningfully during the study process.

An Approach to the Study of Deep/Demanding Texts:

Writing a summary: Write the passage in your own words (10-20% of length). For a longer text, summarize each theme within the text (every 1 to 4 paragraphs, typically). Groups can divide the text into themes and have each person or small group summarize one section. Regardless, read the summaries in order, first forwards and then backwards from the end to the beginning.

Reducing the summary: Reduce each summarized passage to a phrase, e.g., as a chapter title. Repeat the reading forwards and back. Next, have a discussion on the movement of the themes in the passage or text. Try to "see the text from above."

Artistic engagement: Render the summarized segment artistically. This can be in poetry, painting, drawing, music, movement, sculpture, or any other artistic language. It is better to try for the gesture of the passage than for specific details from it, since we are now trying to develop the cognitive feeling, and we are seeking for movement rather than "stuff." When the entire passage or text has been rendered artistically, the participants can read the summaries and the chapter titles as they move from section to section of artistic renderings, even backwards again, and then sit quietly and ponder the artistic rendition and what it "says."

Questions leading to meditative verses: Each participant tries to find a real question, some theme from the text that s/he wants to contemplate further because it feels pregnant with potential meanings that have not yet become perceptible. Then, the whole meaning of the passage is brought full circle back to a meditative text, only this time it is the student's own creation. By trying to express the dynamic meaning of the text in a new dynamic, meditative form, the student can attempt a level of comprehension that approaches the original experience of the author. As lesser lights than the author's we follow, we accept that our verses will not equal the originals, but, nevertheless, we come nearer to the level that Kühlewind calls *cognitive will*. This is the level of cognition in which everything is movement, willed, but with a "soft" will, a receptive and gentle will that is the essence of every truly creative act. Demanding texts are written through this kind of *gentle will*, and should be approached only in the same way. We are trying to become receptive, but actively receptive. The artistic phase served as a *stairway to heaven*, if you will, and now if we are to "walk with the angels," we have to become writers of code, capturing in few signs the wide fields of meaning in which our contemplative process has landed us.

If we follow the gestures of the discursive, the poetic, and the meditative levels of language through this study sequence, we see that the three soul forces have to undergo a kind of inversion:

Thinking, which in the ordinary course of life has an acquisitive nature, has to become intuitive, that is, to merge with the spiritual realities around it.

Feeling, which is ordinarily self-directed in the form of emotions, has to become cognitive and sense the qualities of things.

Will, which is ordinarily an outward, forceful element, has to become the "soft will" of receptive, meditative knowledge.

In this way, the study of demanding texts can become a path of discovery similar in nature to spiritual practice.

ENDNOTE
1. Original lecture given to The Academy for Jewish Religion, November 11, 2012.

The New Impulse of the Second Teachers' Meditation

Introduction

The aim of this article is to demonstrate that the Second Teachers' Meditation represents an essential, new dimension in Rudolf Steiner's guidance to teachers, and that this new dimension adds a crucial layer to what had already been given in the First Teachers' Meditation. It builds from basic concepts of anthroposophy, through the First Teachers' Meditation, to the lectures Steiner gave the teachers in 1923, and concludes with a profound mystery implied in the Second Meditation. I am convinced that this mystery lies at the heart of both the challenges and the opportunities facing the Waldorf movement as it nears the 100th anniversary of its founding.

Background

When the first Waldorf School opened in 1919, after the initial lectures and seminar that constituted the original teacher preparation course, Rudolf Steiner gave the teachers a professional meditation (here called the First Teachers' Meditation). During the years that followed, as he came to visit the teachers in the classrooms and offered them further instructions and guidance during faculty meetings, he sometimes gave them images and short verses, but not a second full-length meditation.

In October of 1923, after visiting the classes in the new academic year, Steiner gave the teachers three lectures and on the following morning brought them a new professional meditation, referring to it as a condensed form of what he had brought in the preceding lectures. When pondered in light of those three lectures, the Second Meditation reveals a profound dimension that might go unnoticed.

I begin by introducing two familiar anthroposophical terms, "threefold" and "fourfold," and proceed to use those as navigational guides, so to speak, throughout the article.

Threefold and Fourfold

The entire foundational text of Waldorf education, *The Foundations of Human Experience*[1] (also published as *Study of Man*), is a meditation on the idea of the human being as a threefold being. This threefold-ness is composed of two contrasting gestures, with an active, dynamic mediating region between them. We see threefold-ness first in the life of the soul (thinking and willing as contrasts, and feeling as the mediating region), then in physiological terms (nerves and blood as contrasts, and the places where they meet as the mediating regions), in spiritual terms (waking and sleeping poles, with dreaming as the middle), and finally in the very shapes of the skeletal system (the round head and linear limbs as contrasting poles, and the ribcage as the middle). Throughout the lectures, and in innumerable lectures on other topics from sociology to medicine to cosmology, Steiner again and again presented pictures of threefold-ness as a fundamental principle in the universe, specifically in the realm of sentient and "I" beings. The Foundation Stone Meditation is the quintessential meditative treatment of the threefold human being. In it, human physiology, soul forces, and the spiritual Trinity are presented as an interrelated triad.

When I speak of a threefold gesture in this article, it is in this sense of two contrasting tendencies and a dynamic middle element. While being principally its own gesture, each of the three elements in a threefold structure contains aspects of the other two. For example, Steiner describes the head as being principally head (round, contained) while having a lower area (the jaw) that resembles a limb in its action and a middle area that has a rhythmic quality (two symmetrical eyes, ears, nostrils), resembling the rhythmic quality of the ribcage.

In the interplay between the three regions, and particularly in the middle realm, new possibilities arise. Towards the end of the Foundation Stone Meditation this is pointed out:

> That good may become
> What from our hearts we found
> And from our heads
> Guide with steadfast willing.

The meditative path yields new possibilities arising out of the inmost heart forces, and the roles of the head and the will are to guide and execute what arises in the heart. In this sense, when we consider the threefold gesture in meditation, it is an inward gesture. It directs the meditative effort towards the transformation of the soul forces of the meditant.

When the initial training course for the first Waldorf teachers moved from the spiritual fundamentals to the application of principles in classroom situations (*Discussions with Teachers*[2]), Steiner introduced a new, fourfold element: the temperaments. He related them to the four elements, to the fourfold human being (physical, etheric, astral, and ego), and concurred with a teacher who related them to musical instruments and to the four gospels (Discussion 2). Steiner instructed the teachers to design their lessons in such a way that each lesson appealed to the four temperaments, and he gave examples for how this could be done. A characteristic feature of the fourfold is that it is composed of a pair of opposites that together form a balance. We can think of fire (warm, dry) as the opposite of water (cold, moist) and earth (cold, dry) as the opposite of air (warm, moist). Similarly, the temperaments can be seen as two pairs of opposites (sanguine-melancholic and choleric-phlegmatic).

As with the threefold gesture, the fourfold is not unique to the pedagogical lectures. In the four elements, the four seasons, the festivals, the four compass directions, and in numerous other connections, fourfold-ness is a principle that is also fundamental in the universe, specifically to the world around the human being (rather than to the soul). When I speak of the fourfold gesture in this article, it is in the sense of a balancing pair of opposites.

From a spiritual-development perspective, the threefold and fourfold gestures direct the soul either inward or outward. Historically, the spiritual streams originating in India tended towards the inner life of thought and meditation. Buddhism, for example, is a path of inner refinement that, while also manifesting in outer conduct, is not focused on knowledge of the outer world. There is nothing of the outer world mentioned in Buddha's Four Noble Truths or the Eightfold Path. By contrast, the spiritual streams of the Middle East (Persia, Egypt, Babylon) focused on knowledge of the starry and earthly worlds, while creating systems of laws to regulate conduct (rather than leaving conduct to be refined by each striving soul). Those cultures created outer edifices that still stand thousands of years later, and we are rightly awe-struck by the precision with which the Egyptians designed a pyramid so that the internal chambers would facilitate observations of specific stars at night, to say nothing of the fact that they (the pyramids) have proved to be so durable.

These two gestures—the threefold and the fourfold—appear in many aspects of anthroposophy. For brevity's sake, I will limit my discussion here to what is most pertinent to the Teachers'

Meditations. We will see how the two gestures find expression in them and in what way the second meditation brings a new element not present in the first.

The First Teachers' Meditation

In shine of sense being
There lives the spirit's will
As wisdom's light outpouring
And inner power concealing.

In the I of my own being
There shines the human will
As thinking's revelation
By its own power supported.

And my own power
With light of cosmic wisdom
Mightfully united
To selfhood shapes me
Who turn myself to high divinity
Seeking powers of illumination.
                    (translation by Arvia M. Ege)

In this meditation we see a threefold gesture come strongly to the fore, while within this gesture, knowledge of the fourfold world is also present. First there is a turning outward and a striving to see the *manifestation* of the world of the senses (the German *Schein*, variously translated as "shine," "glory," "appearance," and "semblance") as a revelation of divine will. Then there is a turning inward to seek the mystery of one's own "I" and will. This denotes a center-and-periphery relationship. In the third stanza the two powers unite to form a new selfhood, rooted in spiritual striving.

This meditation is a powerful inspiration for connecting one's work (or will) with the striving for true knowledge. The Self, in a higher sense, arises out of joining together outer and inner striving. Each part of the meditation (and all of them together) can be remarkably fruitful as one prepares to teach a block or contemplate a child. This meditation can strengthen one's imagination of the teacher as a spiritual striver for whom the horizontal centripetal (striving for self-knowledge) and centrifugal (striving for knowledge of the world) join with the vertical (spiritual practice as a search for higher knowledge) to form a cross of "true north." It encourages making one's spiritual (inner) life and professional (outer) life *one life*.

Lectures of October 1923

In October of 1923, Rudolf Steiner once again came to visit the first Waldorf School. After observing the classes, he gave the teachers three lectures. Those have been published in English as *Deeper Insights into Education: The Waldorf Approach* and more recently as the last three lectures in the new edition of *Balance in Teaching*.[3] The lectures are rather startling in the directness of the criticism leveled at the teachers.

Lecture 1: In the first lecture, Steiner surveyed the history of education from Greece (the gymnast and gymnastics) through Rome (the rhetorician and oratory) to modern times (the professor and abstract science), and he proceeded to demonstrate to the teachers how events in nature need to be taught in order to overcome the deadening effects of modern intellectualism. He talked about the life cycle of the butterfly, connecting the stages of egg, larva, chrysalis, and butterfly with earth, water, air, and fire.

He likewise discussed the life cycle of frogs. Steiner demonstrated the need to connect and weave concepts so that a broad context is given to each individual phenomenon.

It is clear that he was not telling them to continue to do what they had been doing. He was telling them, in effect, that their teaching had become overly intellectual. He demanded that the new pedagogue be a union of the gymnast (educating through the will), the rhetorician (working through the feeling), and the professor, so that the full human being, not just the head, would be addressed by education.

Lecture 2: In the second lecture the criticism became more direct. Steiner flat-out talked of a heavy, depressed mood in the classroom, hinted at artificial enthusiasm, and threw down the gauntlet by speaking of the absolutely crucial need to develop the "Waldorf teacher's consciousness ... which, however, is only possible when, in the field of education, we come to an *actual experience of the spiritual*." (Emphasis mine.) He then proceeded to say that genuine enthusiasm, the most potent force in education, develops only when the teacher acquires an understanding of the healing potential of education.

Again, we must consider that, had the teachers been properly enthusiastic, spiritually insightful, or cognizant of the healing potential of education, there would not have been a need to speak about those topics. The fact that Steiner chose to bring those particular themes (and to add a second teachers' meditation) tells us that, however potent their inner work had been, he clearly saw a need to bring something new. Faculty meetings from the same period, as well as teachers' recollections, point out that Steiner saw significant problems at the school.[4]

Next came a discussion of the fourfold complexes of forces in the human being: movement, nourishment, breathing, and perceiving. It is a fascinating study, but for our purposes we have to leave most of it out. Important for this discussion is the fact that Steiner presented the four complexes of forces as two pairs, with breathing tasked with healing the illnesses brought about by nourishment, and perceiving having to heal the more subtle illnesses brought about by movement. Steiner specifically discussed the ways in which carbon, entering the body through breathing, can unite with various substances in its movement downwards towards the metabolism or upwards towards the head and thinking. These relationships that carbon forms in the body can lead to either health or illness in the human being. He discussed with the teachers how pedagogy could enhance or undermine the health-giving potential of carbon.

[It is very interesting to compare this lecture with a lecture given a week earlier in Dornach at the conclusion of a cycle known in English as "The Four Seasons and the Archangels"[5] (lecture titled "The Working Together of the Four Archangels"). Steiner describes how during each season there is one archangel working cosmically on one half of the earth, while from below, through the earth, the partner archangel works directly into the human being. For example, during the summer Uriel works from above, bringing a sifting, discerning judgment to bear on what human beings have been doing on earth. At the same time, Gabriel works through the earth into the human being's digestive system. The four archangels rotate around the earth through the seasons, taking turns working from above and from below.]

Altogether, both lectures bring a forceful fourfold-ness to the fore. The balancing and healing of the earth and the human being are presented as processes of opposite pairs of forces. In a subtle way, however, Steiner brings a combination of the fourfold and the threefold to bear in both instances, since a healthy, balanced condition is an active, dynamic balance of contrasting forces.

47

Lecture 3: The third lecture to the teachers was given on the evening after the second one. In it Rudolf Steiner once again took up the theme of carbon's "behavior" in the body and in nature, but with a startling, new twist. He told the teachers that proper pedagogy sows seeds of health and truth that can bear fruit many years later, even if outer circumstances offer great resistance. He went so far as to say that, even under tyranny, a teacher working with the right thoughts and the proper enthusiasm can sow the seeds of future health for the child. He ended by calling this health-giving pedagogy a union of the teacher with the task of the archangel Michael, and contrasting it with the dry, intellectual scientific knowledge that is practiced under the auspices of Ahriman. We know that Michael, as the countenance of the Christ, is not merely opposed to Ahriman but stands between Ahriman and Lucifer. We will come to the pedagogical aspects of the Luciferic danger later. In this lecture, however, Steiner contrasted the Michaelic education for which he was advocating with the intellectual, Ahrimanic tendencies he had witnessed in the classrooms.

On the following morning, Steiner gave the teachers their new professional meditation. We should bear in mind the thread: intellectualism can be overcome by pedagogical enthusiasm; enthusiasm is born of an understanding of education's healing potential; the healing consists of helping to balance opposing forces within the human constitution.

The Second Teachers' Meditation

Spirit beholding
Turn deeply seeing within.
Heart-warm touching
Touch upon tender soul being.
In expectant spirit beholding,
In strong-hearted, fine soul touching,
There, weaving, is consciousness-being.
Consciousness-being,
Which from the above and the below
Of the human being
Binds cosmic brightness
To earthly darkness.

Spirit beholding
Heart-warm touching
Behold and touch
In Man's inner being,
Weaving cosmic brightness
In reigning earthly darkness
My own
Human formative force
Engendering
Power creating
Will sustaining
Self.

The gesture presented in the first part of this meditation is similar to the one in the first teachers' meditation. Two contrasting gestures—spirit beholding (though the German word *blicken* means something closer to "glancing" or "glimpsing" than to "beholding") and heart-warm touching—allow for a third (uniquely human) element: consciousness-being, to bind cosmic brightness and earthly darkness. It is actually two threefold gestures, one of human effort and one of cosmic-earthly relationships, with consciousness-being common to both.

With the second part of this meditation, however, an essentially new element is introduced: the two activities—beholding (or glancing) and touching—are again invoked, then intensified,[6] and now directed in a wholly surprising direction (Man's inner being) in order to find "my own ... Self." The sentence there would read:

> Behold and touch [both on the intensified level]
> In Man's inner being...
> My own
> Self.

In between "My own" and "Self" are three effects that the meditant's activities can generate, thereby "weaving cosmic brightness in reigning earthly darkness," engender human formative forces, create power, and sustain the will. A critical question is: generate in whom?

When we consider what Steiner said about the healing potential of education in the context of the four complexes of forces, this sentence assumes a remarkable meaning:

The "ordinary" spiritual striving of the human being brings about the birth of a higher Self; when that Self is sought in the inner being of the other, it generates *in the other* (the child, in this case, or perhaps one's colleague) those three healing effects, and weaves cosmic brightness in earthly darkness in a whole new way. This healing dimension is not present in the First Meditation, and I would argue that it is an essential, new quality in the Second

Meditation. It is a manifestation, within pedagogy, of the central task of humanity.

The True Self

At this point it would be helpful to introduce a differentiation of the three selves in Rudolf Steiner's work: the lower self, the higher Self, and the True Self.[7]

The lower self is the familiar "me-consciousness" that is based on our identification with our physical body. It is the self that has to be transformed, the aspect susceptible to temptations of all kinds.

The higher Self is the source of our capacity for creativity (the "I"). It can be thought of as an opening rather than a "thing," the psycho-spiritual vortex, so to speak, that allows us to bring something new into the world. In inner development this vortex is cultivated consciously, while in other situations it can beget new creations spontaneously. (Not all creative people are spiritual students.)

The True Self is the archetypal capacity for love, referred to in Steiner's work as The Christ. Steiner describes how the Christ event brought together the Buddha stream (which is connected with what we have called the inward, threefold soul gesture) with the Zarathustra stream (which is connected with what we have called the outward, know-the-world-in-its-fourfold-ness gesture). Before Christ, a human being could undergo initiation in one of those paths, but not in both during one lifetime. The Christ event united the two streams, and since that time it has been possible to find the higher Self through both paths in one lifetime. When that is done, when the world's wisdom and the essence of the Self are both reached so that the human being is in its inmost Self and at the same time in the depths of world being, the True Self can also be reached if, in that moment, what the higher Self brings into the world is love. The capacity to actuate love through the innermost uniting with the depths of the outer is the moment when "Not I, but Christ in me" is realized.

If we look at the Second Teachers' Meditation with this perspective in mind, we see in it two gestures coming together: on the one side, the threefold inner path, uniting above and below through transformed human consciousness; on the other, an intensification of the initiation efforts leading to a new gesture: the enhanced beholding-touching effort joining with the self-higher Self union to meet the fourfold reality of the other human being.

By turning towards the other (the child, with his need for healing, in this case, or perhaps the colleague) and seeking my Self in his inner being (not, crucially, in *my* inner being), the possibility arises that my creative capacity, my Self, can be brought into service of the needs and being of the other. Any creative activity that is generated out of *that* Self is the healing, redemptive activity that Steiner exhorted the teachers to practice as the source of genuine pedagogical enthusiasm. Here my Self is found in the depths of the inner being of the other. The innermost and the depths of the outer are one. Creativity practiced as Love. The True Self.

Historical Anecdote

In his book, *Rudolf Steiner: A Biography*,[8] Christoph Lindenberg relates that in 1922 a government inspector came to visit the first Waldorf School in Stuttgart. The inspector's report was quite critical of the school, pointing to several deficiencies. The teachers reacted bitterly, but Rudolf Steiner would have none of their complaints. He said that the state inspector clearly wanted to avoid harming the school, but that what he (the inspector) had seen could not be ignored. Steiner further stated that he was in agreement with much of what the inspector had written. He brought up the notion that what is good (the curriculum) also has to be applied well, and that this application required a certain enthusiasm, an inner engagement that had disappeared from the school little by little. We can note that in the lectures delivered the following year, and described above, the theme of pedagogical enthusiasm is taken up vigorously.

Steiner died in March of 1925. In the late fall of that year, the state once again came to inspect the Waldorf School. This time, the report (as quoted in Lindenberg, p.528) stated:

> Anyone who comes in contact with the Waldorf School recognizes immediately that a unique group of teachers is leading this school. Their connection to one another appears to be exemplary. They serve each other in love; each radiates energy and receives energy in return; there is no indication of trivial in-fighting, jealousy, or envy. …The students sincerely love their teachers, who, rejecting all forms of physical punishment, work to form the body, soul, and spirit of each child entrusted to them through love, goodness, and wisdom, and their own exemplary actions.

The fact that the two reports, so different in what they describe, came before and after the giving of the Second Teachers' Meditation is, of course, not in itself proof of anything. But we can take the second report as a description of what we should all strive to create in Waldorf schools. And we can approach the Second Teachers' Meditation knowing that it played at least a part in moving the first Waldorf School from the impression it made in 1922 to the one made in 1925.

Practical Considerations

Many Waldorf teachers practice creativity. It is common to find teachers writing poetry, music, or pedagogical stories; making beautiful chalkboard drawings and paintings; creating new games; designing projects of various kinds; and so forth. This tradition is commendable and certainly preferable to stale and set-in-their-ways teachers who only repeat what they themselves (or others) have done previously. Creativity, as discussed earlier, is often a manifestation of the higher Self. (There are darker sources of creativity as well, but what may inspire a heavy metal band is not what Waldorf teachers draw upon.)

Teachers who create are more apt to look forward to seeing their students; they yearn to share what they have done, and one senses in their whole demeanor freshness and youthful vigor. If there is a shadow to this creative effort, it is that it can supersede pedagogical considerations because the teacher is caught up in the joy and satisfaction of his/her creation. The act of "birthing," which is selfless, is followed by a sense of ownership, which is not.

An example is a teacher who is so keen to produce a play (he has written) exactly according to his artistic imagination that rehearsals become either tyrannical or ecstatic in mood. The outcome may look wonderful to the audience, but the process did not serve the students as well as it might have. The students became secondary to the play; this may be justified in a professional theater production, but it is not a pedagogically sound process. We see here how a creative impulse is marred by the egotistical shadow that can often accompany such efforts. Similar situations (in which students become secondary) can be seen whenever the teacher becomes personally invested in the outcome of the children's artistic endeavor rather than focusing on the children themselves. This can be true of the beauty in the lesson books, the sound of the class' choral singing and/or recitation, especially when preparing for a performance, or even the way in which the children are led through the hall during an assembly.

Whenever the teacher's self (as opposed to Self) guides the action, the me-consciousness of the teacher overcomes the good intentions that his/her (self-less) inner pedagogue had in the first place. What begins as an exciting creative process veers away from service and towards egotism. I believe that if heaviness and depression are the results of excessively intellectual teaching, then euphoric, ecstatic, and/or tyrannical moods, even if they appear only in subtle ways, are the results of creative efforts placed too much at the service of the teacher's own need for self-fulfillment.

American Waldorf schools, at least the grade schools, do not often suffer from the depressive, overly intellectual mood described in Steiner's lectures of October 1923; the opposing danger to which I refer above is a more common phenomenon. I leave it to my high school colleagues to assess the situation in their domain. However, if we consider these depressive-ecstatic dangers as being two poles of a threefold picture, then the two types of un-pedagogical modes are not as far apart as they might seem, at least not when what we are after is a healing education. As Steiner says in the second of these lectures, healthy or unhealthy should replace true or false as the quintessential question in education. Unhealthy in one mode can have a hidden partner in the other unhealthy mode, and the finger that points at the overly intellectual may belong to the excessively ecstatic artist. Health-giving does not point fingers, but rather draws the necessary contributions from either pole—"necessary" for the child, that is.

The Second Teachers' Meditation provides the counter impulse to both the first (depressive) and second (ecstatic) modes. When the inner life of the teacher is divorced from the needs for healing of his/her students, the twin dangers (and others besides) have an easier access to both his inner life and his outward conduct. When the teachers' meditation itself includes turning towards the inner being of the other as the source of one's creative potential, Michael, the countenance of the True Self, is at hand. If we place the child's need for healing at the mainspring of our creative action, what comes thereof may well be the water of life. It is in this sense that we can come to an actual experience of the spiritual in our pedagogical work, finding the genuine, healing enthusiasm of which we and the world stand in such great need.

ENDNOTES

1. Rudolf Steiner, *The Foundations of Human Experience*, Great Barrington, MA: Anthroposophic Press, 1996.
2. Rudolf Steiner, *Discussions with Teachers*, Great Barrington, MA: Anthroposophic Press, 1997.
3. Rudolf Steiner, *Balance in Teaching*, Great Barrington, MA: Anthroposophic Press, 2007.
4. Rudolf Steiner, *Faculty Meetings with Rudolf Steiner*, Hudson, NY: Anthroposophic Press, 1998.
5. Rudolf Steiner, *The Four Seasons and the Archangels*, Forest Row, UK: Rudolf Steiner Press, 1996.
6. There is no English equivalent to the difference between *blicken* and *erblicke* or the similar difference between *tasten* and *ertaste*, but the "er" points to an intensification of the activity, usually from within outwards.
7. For this distinction I owe Sergei Prokofieff gratitude. He presents a thorough description of this theme in his book, *The First Class of the Michael School and Its Christological Foundations*. This book is available only to members of the First Class of the School for Spiritual Science through the author's secretary: sekretariatSP@

goetheanum.ch. The description of the three selves in this article is my own; Prokofieff's treatment of this important topic is far deeper and more thorough than what is presented here.

8. Christoph Lindenberg, *Rudolf Steiner: A Biography,* Great Barrington, MA: SteinerBooks, 2012.

Between Our Gods and Our Demons
Human Encounter in the Light of Anthroposophy

This article is based on a keynote lecture given at the opening of the 2017 AWSNA Teachers Conference, held at the Cedarwood Waldorf School in Portland, OR.

When Melanie Reiser, AWSNA Executive Director for Membership, asked me if I would speak at the opening of this conference, she read me our Association's Shared Principle #7. It begins with the words: "Waldorf schools are self-administered. This work is strengthened by cultivating a shared anthroposophical understanding of social interactions." She said, "Talk about what that means."

My mind quickly turned to my earliest days as a Waldorf teacher. There were two teachers in the school I joined, and every week during the faculty meeting a strange ritual would unfold: Some topic or other would be up for discussion; sooner or later, one of the two would take a stand, usually in strong, confident words. With the predictability of a Swiss watch, the other would take the opposite point of view. It didn't matter whether we were talking about a specific child, planning a festival, or debating where teachers should park their cars in the morning. Sometimes it seemed that one of them would try to take the point of view that the other usually espoused, as if to make nice. No matter: The other would contradict his usual approach just for the occasion, as if saying, "I usually stand for X, and you stand for Y, but today, since you suggest X, I must advocate for Y." It became clear to me that the topics were not really what mattered;

rather, it was the encounter between these two that had its own gesture. The consequence of these weekly debates was that the meetings often felt both predictable and exhausting. I would even say predictably exhausting. I would like to leave this little image, surely one that is not entirely unfamiliar to many of you, as an example of one kind of encounter.

The other example I want to present is from a College of Teachers meeting I attended several years later. The purpose of the meeting was to review the work of the College during the previous school year. A colleague said something deeply significant: "Two things really strike me about our meetings: The first is that they always surprise me. We find new ideas and solutions that no one seemed to have had when the meeting began, and I personally often leave feeling that I have more energy than I had when I came in." So that's a different kind of encounter, with radically different results. I would like to posit that surprise, in the good sense, and renewed energy are two hallmarks of the encounters we should foster.

Back to Melanie and Shared Principle #7: I pondered the wording, particularly the "anthroposophical understanding of social interactions." It struck me, eventually, that anthroposophy has one essential contribution to make to the study of social interactions. It is strikingly simple to articulate: Spiritual beings interpose themselves between us as we meet. Whatever techniques, practices, policies, and structures we can find helpful from the world outside Waldorf education, this essential insight will always form a dimension that must be taken into account. Spiritual beings interpose themselves between us as we meet.

Mainstream psychology and sociology books that have looked into the area of social interactions have not been able to explore this possibility, and for three reasons: first, because the requisite conceptual framework that would allow for this contribution is missing. Therefore, second, the language that would allow for an articulation of insights is missing or ignored. And third, the capacities that are needed for meaningful research to unfold are nowhere to be found, since no one recognizes that they are needed in the first place. In other words, given that spiritual beings are not acknowledged in the mainstream, they do not enter its conceptual framework, its terminology, or its tools of research and analysis.

When we undertake the task of leading an organization as a team, clarity about, and a conscious cultivation of, the relationship with spiritual beings is an ever-urgent pair of challenges. We will first look at the historical development of our relationship with certain spiritual beings and then consider a few suggestions for cultivating healthy human encounters in light of the presence of those beings.

Soul Encounters as a Particular Challenge

The image of the human in anthroposophy is of a threefold being: body, soul, and spirit. I will focus here solely on the second aspect of the human constitution, namely the soul.[1]

Because they are often entangled in a web of emotions, difficult soul encounters challenge us in ways that can feel overwhelming and insurmountable. They lack the clarity of spiritual principles, and so remain nebulous, yet they carry a powerful surge of emotional intensity.

Rudolf Steiner describes two phases in the relationship of the "I", the Self, to the lower members of the human constitution. The first phase entails an unconscious, the second a conscious set of transformations. The first phase produces an elaboration of the lower members (developed for us by spiritual beings) into three soul layers. The second phase produces three layers of spirit. I would like to briefly describe the stages of the first phase and to characterize the resulting soul layers. In anthroposophical nomenclature, all of these layers have particular names. My language here, to the extent possible, will avoid these names in favor of signature gestures, by which I mean the activities that most characterize each layer. My intention is not to deny the validity of the usual terminology, but to encourage both you and me to avoid familiar words that we, often too easily, assume we understand, perhaps more than we actually do.

Historical Context

At the outset of the transformational process just mentioned, the human constitution includes three facets that Rudolf Steiner called the physical, etheric, and astral "bodies"; I should note that the English translation "body" for the German Leib can be problematic in discussing the etheric and the astral, since they lack obvious physical characteristics. (The German *Leib* is not as problematic, given that its original signification is less grounded in the corporeal—the way the word used in relation to the animal and human body, *Körper*, is; *Leib* is closer to the use of "body" in English in expressions such as "body of knowledge.") The first is a physical body. We can think of it as the material level that we share with all mineral, living, and sentient beings. The second is the life body, which we can think of as the level we share with living organisms that grow and reproduce, namely plants and animals. The third Steiner called the astral or soul body. It is the level we share with all sentient beings, namely animals. Its signature gestures are movement, both inner (as in a response to stimuli and circumstances) and outer (autonomous displacement that plants cannot achieve). Another way of saying this is that beings endowed with an astral body exhibit some degree of consciousness.

When the human Self, or "I," was introduced into the evolution, it began interacting with these existing bodies. These interactions were initially completely unconscious. And although they have produced increasingly conscious results, as we shall see, these interactions only recently began, themselves, growing more wakeful within us.

The Desiring Soul; The Spirit of Fun and Freedom; Illness, Suffering, and Pain

At first, during a period that Rudolf Steiner calls Lemuria, the Self began interacting with what we have termed the astral body. Merely instinctual, animal-like responses to stimuli grew more individualized. People could begin to like and dislike aspects of their environment in ways that differed from their peers. Rudimentary personality traits began to emerge.

At this point, an important spiritual intervention took place. Up until then, only benevolent spiritual beings were involved in earth evolution. But now, adversarial spiritual beings at a level equivalent to what Western traditions call angels developed a different relationship with humanity. Collectively, we can refer to these spirits in the singular as The Spirit of Fun and Freedom. Genesis depicts it as the serpent; elsewhere it is called the Devil, or Lucifer. It introduced the possibility of error into human conduct. The result was, on the one hand, a greater level of separation of humanity from its divine origins, and therefore freedom for the individual human being; and, on the other, the development of desires, cravings, and lust for sensations.

It was the first elaboration of the human soul—we can call it the Desiring Soul. Think of the moment when you meet a person and feel either an irresistible desire or an equally strong repulsion toward that person. On a more trivial level, you open a catalogue that just arrived in the mail, or surf a commercial website, and suddenly you cannot live another moment without owning an item that five minutes earlier you did not even know existed. Or you see something that someone else has and you really, REALLY want it.

An important characteristic of the Desiring Soul is that it is inherently insatiable. No amount of goods, food, or pleasure is ever enough for more than a brief interval of time.

In order to mitigate the results of what The Spirit of Fun and Freedom wrought, the benevolent spiritual forces had to introduce illness, suffering, and pain into the life of humanity, so that we would not utterly succumb to the temptations of the senses. This may sound cruel to the modern mind, but we can also think of it as being given the opportunity to learn to live with consequences. Other terms for that are growing up or maturing. Like a young person coming into adulthood, one has to learn there is a price for bingeing on anything, and sometimes even for trying just a little taste. A hangover after a night of drinking is one common example of how our desire for sensations can result in adverse consequences. Addictions of all kinds provide more examples.

The Explaining/Planning Soul;
The Spirit of the Machine; Karma

The next step in evolution involved the Self penetrating and unconsciously transforming the life body. This took place in the period that Steiner terms Atlantis. Living organisms grow in regulated, law-governed ways, which shows us that there is an intelligible pattern governing their life cycles. This pattern is coded, so to speak, into the life body. When the Self finished "working through" the life body, the result was a second layer of soul, one that we can designate The Explaining or Planning Soul. To get a feeling for it, we can imagine that the Desiring Soul wishes for some item or experience. It is the role of the Planning Soul to figure out how to satisfy the wish of the Desiring Soul. For example, we can plan on buying this item, stealing it, or killing our neighbor in order to get it. All three would achieve the desired result, and for the Planning Soul there isn't yet a particular preference for one over the other, except expediency. In the realm of knowledge acquisition, the Explaining Soul does just that: It explains things, which means replacing mysterious phenomena (e.g., nature's) with models that are easier to comprehend. The entire edifice of natural science is the glorious, and problematic, triumph of the Explaining Soul, essentially replacing the mysteries of nature with mathematical formulations. It is immensely satisfying to feel that we know what something "really is," even if, for example, we are not much closer to understanding the nature of pleasure when we say that pleasure "really is" nothing but the body secreting certain hormones (e.g., serotonin, oxytocin, or dopamine). We have just turned our gaze to where the street lamp is lighting a section of the sidewalk, even if it isn't where we lost our keys, or at least not most of them. Still, we are left with the satisfying illusion of knowing. In effect, we have translated the world into the language of mathematics, and now a blind person can understand color just as well as a seeing person, because "color really is nothing but an angle of refraction, or a wavelength, that can be expressed mathematically." The same goes for all the other senses and their sensations, and even for consciousness itself. We think that we have explained the senses, but in reality we have only explained them away. The world disappears, and all that's left is math.

When the Explaining/Planning Soul came into being, there was a second intervention of spiritual beings, this time of the adversarial level equivalent to that of the archangels. We can name them, in the singular, The Spirit of the Machine. The Persians, as well as anthroposophists, name it Ahriman. Others call it Satan. Initially, this spirit's influence led to the possibility of what we call sin. Sin differs from error in that the former is deliberate. Human beings could now know in advance that they were violating the intended order of the universe. A second consequence of the presence of the Spirit of the Machine was that knowledge of the spiritual origins of existence was gradually lost, and people could no longer see beyond the senses. We can appreciate, therefore, how materialism could develop.

To mitigate the influence of the Spirit of the Machine, the benevolent forces introduced death and the law of karma. We shall return to death a little later. But karma is really a wonderful thing! We usually think of it as the source of all manner of difficulties, but we should be eternally grateful that it exists, for it allows for the balancing of sins. Imagine if your sins were written into your being in such a way that it would be impossible to make matters right. Next time you find yourself in a karmic knot, be glad and thankful for it. You may not be able to untie it yet, but at least you have the opportunity to try.

The Understanding/Empathetic Soul; The Spirits of Darkness; AHAVA

The third chapter in the Self's unconscious transforming of the lower members was its penetration of the physical body. It is still ongoing and has been bringing a third soul facet into existence. This facet we can designate the Understanding or Empathetic Soul. Its chief attribute is that it can serve as a moral compass. In the example I gave earlier, the Planning Soul can find different ways of satisfying the cravings and wishes of the Desiring Soul. How would one choose which of these ways is best? For the materialistic-thinking Planning Soul, expediency is the only arbiter. But what of ethics? If the Planning Soul can say, "true or false, fast or slow," the Understanding Soul can tell, and FEEL, the difference between good and evil. It is the soul that can understand, rather than merely explain, and that can empathize with another human being. After the increasing distance from the phenomena that the Desiring Soul and Explaining Soul have produced, the Empathetic Soul can re-connect with phenomena, this time without disappearing completely into a dreamy or sleepy state of consciousness. "I" can understand "you," rather than merely feeling attraction or repulsion, as with the Desiring Soul, or explain you (using extrinsic measures) to myself, as with the Explaining Soul.

There is also a third intervention of adversarial spiritual beings that is beginning, and this one has a particular twist. These beings are the adversarial equivalents to the spiritual hierarchy designated in Christian esotericism as the Archai. While the benevolent Archai bestowed the Self on humanity, these adversarial counterparts work in precisely the opposite direction. They encourage human beings to divert the understanding capacities (which the Self has been developing) in order to manipulate others in purely egotistical ways. Sociopathy and psychopathy are examples of this type of action, and orgiastic behaviors, for example, point toward a future in which some people will gear their entire lives toward incessant sensual pleasure. The sociopath has a keen understanding of others, but does not care about their wellbeing. The psychopath is similarly insightful, but goes even further by actually enjoying the pain he can inflict. The twist in the narrative here is that, according to Rudolf Steiner, the benevolent spiritual powers cannot help us find redemption for acts committed under the influence of these new adversarial forces, which he names (using an old term for the Archai) the Asuras; every time we choose the path of pure egotism, a sliver of our divine Self is lost to darkness. This is a new reality in human evolution, and means that we are now increasingly capable of self-annihilation. It is darkness, the likes of which humanity has never encountered before.

But where a great darkness appears, a great light must also be present. This light I would like to designate AHAVA, the acronym for "Archetype of Human Amity, Verity, and Altruism." Conveniently, AHAVA means "love" in Hebrew, and we can think of "the archetype of the human capacity for love" as another name or designation for AHAVA. I will use "the Love Impulse" to describe what AHAVA is trying to help us develop. Rudolf Steiner referred to it, in a term that was less problematic for his milieu than it is for our time, as the "Christ Impulse."

According to Steiner, there was a moment in history when AHAVA joined the earthly, human stream of being for a brief period. It penetrated the lower sheaths, or bodies, of a human being and, as a human being, shed blood into the earth as it died. This love-infused blood turned into life forces (ether), and the earth itself began, for the first time, to radiate light into the cosmos. AHAVA moved its sphere of action into the sheaths surrounding the earth, and the light associated with Love began radiating as the earth's own emanation. This light was not yet physical, but if human beings take this Love Impulse into themselves, it will increasingly condense into physical light until the earth itself will become a new sun!

The Etherization of Blood and the Love Impulse

As if the idea of helping to make the earth into a new sun is not inspiring enough, Rudolf Steiner also says that every human heart turns a portion of the blood that passes through it into a fine stream of life (or etheric) forces that flows upwards into the head. When human beings take up the Love Impulse into themselves, the individual stream of etherized blood joins the etherized stream of the Love Impulse, and completely new capacities can arise in the soul. Those capacities are key elements of any potential progress for humanity, and, I suggest, for the potential survival and success of Waldorf schools. They entail, among other things, direct perception of spiritual realities and an ability to act out of the highest moral ideals.

Human Encounter on the Three Levels; Proposed Practices

Thus far we have surveyed an evolutionary process and followed the appearance and influence of various spiritual beings, both benevolent and adversarial. It is time to "get down to brass tacks," as the saying goes: What can we do in a school context in order to facilitate healthy human encounters, knowing that our demons and our gods, as my title suggests, are both eager for our cooperation?

I would like to take each of the three soul facets, or members, characterize its typical appearance in human relationships, and propose an approach that concentrates on the elements that promote health and wellbeing—in other words, a salutogenic approach.

The Desiring Soul

The two archetypal gestures of the Desiring Soul are attraction and repulsion. A new colleague or parent comes into view, and one feels a strong attraction toward this person, or perhaps a strong revulsion. In our culture, it is not acceptable to express these sentiments. I don't think that school communities would benefit if they encouraged verbal expression of the animal-level desires and revulsions that we might feel toward one another. The point here is not to externalize what might ordinarily be expressed only in anonymous online chat rooms. There are not only humane grounds for restraint, but legal ones as well.

However, simply suppressing the lower impulses of the Desiring Soul is not a good practice either, if it remains the only thing we do. Suppression leads to repression, and repression leads to illness. You can sit in a faculty meeting and find yourself wondering why on earth tensions run so high when the topic is seemingly so banal. The same two or three individuals seem intent on clashing with one another regardless of the topic, as in the example with which I started. The opposite can also happen: People agree with one another based on sympathy, or even attraction, and yet the root of their agreement is not the topic at hand or the wellbeing of the school. When people manage to sublimate their attraction and repulsion completely, physical and/ or emotional illness can arise. We don't overcome a lower aspect of ourselves by pretending it does not exist.

In short, the two extremes of repression and expression are not healthy for us, nor for the school. What I would like to suggest is that there is a way of processing the impulses of the Desiring Soul, a way that can be healthy. By this I mean engagement with the arts, specifically in what I would call chamber arts: eurythmy, chorus, speech chorus, drama, music making, and so on. There is a whole field of artistic endeavors, some extant and some waiting to be developed, that would allow teams to work through the impulses of the Desiring Soul so that beauty can emerge out of the process. Since the Spirit of Fun and Freedom is also a key inspiration for artistic creativity, we would be using this Spirit's gifts to neutralize his malevolent influence!

An essential benefit of chamber arts is that they provide a strong impetus for recognizing the spiritual in our fellow human beings. Artistic processes, when done well, move people through obstacles and long-established patterns, and allow them to grow. When we witness someone growing, we know that we are in the presence of a "human becoming" entity. This experience should always leave us hopeful: What is problematic today may change in time. As long as we are hopeful, progress is possible. The main problem with our patterns of desire and revulsion is that, especially with the latter, we assume permanence. But when our "enemy" has overcome an artistic blockage or, better yet, helped us overcome one of our own, a layer of enmity is shed. Over time, sufficient layers can be shed so the two of us can see the better aspects of each other that were previously hidden from our view. Real conversations, verbal or through correspondence, are another way of overcoming these impulses. They are seeds of the future social art of conversation. A striking and very moving example is the late-life correspondence between Thomas Jefferson and John Adams.

In short, I would like to throw down something of a gauntlet here to my art-teaching colleagues: There is a whole field of exercises that you can develop to help teams healthily process the lower impulses of the soul.

I want to be clear that individual artistic work can also be helpful. I have written a lot of poetry to process my life's events. But individual work helps an individual. Chamber work helps those who are in the chamber, which, in the context of the current discussion, is the relevant group within the school. But another aspect of its efficacy is that it invites the spiritual beings that support harmony and collaboration to be active for the duration people strive together artistically.

The Planning/Explaining Soul

The signature gestures of the Explaining Soul have in common that they are past-oriented and replace genuine encounter with analyses and prescriptions of all kinds. Because the birth of the Explaining Soul was accompanied by the possibility of sin, schools and organizations have introduced "sin prevention" programs: policies and procedures! This leads to a safer environment, but also to a stilted and warmth-less one. Every bureaucrat says, "That's the policy. I did not make it, I just administer it." The policy was no doubt created because someone did something that had the "flavor" of sin, therefore having some kind of justification for it. I am not suggesting that policies and procedures have no place in a school. But they do present a new kind of challenge by introducing general rules for all, thereby limiting activities of the human being as an individual and handling complex realities with a one-size-fits-all approach.

A second common gesture of the Explaining Soul is the dissection of another person by the use of psychoanalytic language. This language is invariably past-oriented. Parents or food or some trauma are held responsible for something that a person did or for the way he or she is behaving. Again, there may be some justification for this approach, but it comes with the danger that we distance ourselves from the other, and most importantly that we feel superior to the other. Since we think we know why she behaves in this particular way, we can respond with empathy, but all too often we adopt the self-congratulatory mood of seeing the other "from above." I would like to suggest three practices that can help us work with the gifts of the Explaining Soul in order to neutralize its deleterious effects:

1. The first is enlivened study of inspired texts. The hallmarks of enlivened study are that it is experiential, context-rich, and deed-oriented. When we merely read a text in a faculty meeting, the effect is minimal and sometimes even negative. Study is best begun by bringing in an experience; just as we know from the classroom that beginning with the will and proceeding through feeling to thinking is the best way to go, so also in the faculty study.

Healthy study is also context-rich. It arises out of and, in turn, creates context and relationships. Anything, even an anthroposophical concept, studied in isolation is a lie. For example, the cultural, political, and location-specific circumstances of Steiner's lectures are important; we can also follow up a reading with a discussion of how the themes he develops may need to be articulated in terms of our own circumstances. It is inconceivable to me that Steiner would be saying the same things in the same language a hundred years later. He was the consummate innovator and revitalizer of culture; how would he have developed his themes in light of what has transpired since he first brought them forth?

Finally, study should be deed-oriented. We should ask ourselves: What is indicated by this study for our work? How do we translate the inspiration of the text into action?

2. The second practice or "cure" for the Explaining Soul is a study of nature as a text. For example, the works of two of our colleagues, Craig Holdrege and Dennis Klocek, demonstrate instances of research into the meaning of natural phenomena.[2]

When we seek for meaning, as opposed to explanation, we learn to read nature as a text. A text implies a creative force, an author, and this sense helps us overcome an ailment that the Spirit of the Machine has infected us with: the estrangement from our divine origins.

3. The third "cure" is the study of projective geometry. The Explaining Soul typically traffics in mathematical explanations that replace phenomena with numbers. Projective geometry is a mathematical field that requires imaginative capacities if it is to be understood. It is, if you will, the redemption of our relationships with mathematics. It begins with familiar geometric notions, but quickly moves into dimensions that must be grasped imaginatively. The soul has to dance, so to speak, between observable spaces and familiar laws, on the one hand, and specifically and precisely imagined spaces and phenomena, on the other. We learn to see with the mind's eye, and even draw what only the mind can actually see. Thus, the mathematical mindset that once estranged us from the non-physical worlds becomes a gateway back into these worlds.

The Empathetic Soul

Encounters that originate with the Empathetic Soul are most easily characterized as those moments when someone else sees us. Beyond gender, race, age, appearance, status, and all the other veils that hide us from one another, we are, all of us, human beings, each one of us a species unto ourselves. When another person can see us, we are neither simply attractive or repulsive, nor are we explained through some pre-existing model (not even an anthroposophic one). While these interpretations will, no doubt, play into what another sees, he or she can see something genuine—us, or something of us. It is an exhilarating moment!

It is just as exhilarating when we are the ones who manage to see—really see—another human being. On the few occasions in my life when that has happened, I have felt like Adam in the Garden of Eden. There is such simplicity and purity in this kind of encounter; it leaves your heart open and receptive, without the veils that customarily come between people. The question then arises: What happens now?

When one person sees another, there are usually only two basic choices to be made: to love or to hurt. I don't mean sensual love; I mean that you have seen another human being, including his or her golden qualities and less-than-golden needs. To the needs you can respond with whatever it is you have to offer. To the other's golden qualities you respond by calling them forth. Or you can put a hook into the need and begin to manipulate. You can also ignore, remain indifferent, but that is just another way of hurting. And you can try to undermine the golden qualities.

We have all met people of both kinds of resolve. In the presence of someone who has seen another and chosen love, we feel peace. With those who lust for power and who utilize their insights for control and manipulation, we can feel helpless. They are far too clever and skilled for us to meet head on. We can sense that ultimately only love can counter their power. It cannot redeem them, but it can serve as a countermeasure within individuals and communities. The opportunity for love to build momentum in our situation may take time. In the meantime, they can do a lot of damage.

As I mentioned before, there is no direct remediation of the dark impulses we are talking about. But if love is ultimately the antidote, there are a couple of practices that we can take up in order to strengthen our relationship with the Love Impulse. There are others, too, but we are focusing now on collegial relationships.

1. The first is biography work. This is a fairly well-developed field of study in our circles, with people who are skilled at facilitating excellent processes. Entering attentively into the images of another's life and then taking those into our sleep life for several days can go a long way toward building a real feeling of brotherhood and sisterhood.

2. The second is meditation. The path toward the Love Impulse needs to be taken up within each one of us. As Steiner developed this work, an essential aspect of it is that we first build up a picture, and then we allow what we have achieved to disappear, to die, as it were. Only the force we had built up in the process of forming the image remains. Apart from the value of meditative work as a spiritual path of knowledge, the practice of letting something die within us is a profound step toward Love.

When death is approached without fear, anger, or resentment, it can be the most amazingly graceful moment in the whole of life. We can "gift" our dying to those around us as their opportunity to care. In the realm of ideas, death means renouncing our ownership and attachment to what originally came to us, allowing it to be owned and revised by the group. And when we see another person, with her physical, emotional, karmic, or any other illness, we can ask ourselves: "Were she on death's bed, would I love her?" If the answer is yes, and few of us would choose to attack or ignore a person on death's bed, the next question is: "Why should I wait until she is on death's bed to love her?"

We find, when approaching our fellow human being with the mindset that "Love shouldn't wait," that the twin experiences of surprise and invigoration meet us all the time. Just like a good College meeting!

ENDNOTES

1. For a summary of Steiner's threefold image of the human being, see my "Contribution to the Study of the First Core Principle." *Research Bulletin* 19(2): 54–57, 2014.

2. Craig Holdrege's work encompasses plant and animal studies, and can be found at www.natureinstitute.org; Dennis Klocek studies a wide range of natural phenomena. His work can be accessed at www.coros.org.

REFERENCES

Steiner, Rudolf. *The Deed of Christ and the Opposing Spiritual Forces* (GA 107).

_____. *The Etherization of the Blood* (GA 130).

_____. *From Jesus to Christ* (GA 131).

_____. *The Gospel of St. John and Its Relation to the Other Gospels* (GA 112).

55473006R00047

Made in the USA
Middletown, DE
16 July 2019